WONDERFUL AFRICAN ANIMALS

AMADOU BA

WONDERFUL AFRICAN ANIMALS

Children's Book

AMADOU BA

AB Alke Bulan Editions

Foreword

The Africa landscapes still inspire tourists and all lovers of fauna and flora. Many animals in Africa are deeply rooted in their collective imaginary. Africa animals are distinguished by their great diversity, their incredible qualities, and their role in African societies as well as in the environment. The vast African continent, cradle of humanity, also occupies a prominent place for the development of the most astounding species. The Sahel and savannah, as well as the forest and deserts of the continent are home to many animals, from the biggest such as elephants, giraffe, lion, zebra, etc. to the smallest species. In this book you will learn more about African animals, what they mean to Africans and what Africans think of them.

The lion

I'm lion. I'm the bush killer. I dominate all animals. When I roar, all hearts tremble. I have several names and qualifications depending on where I am in Africa. They call me lion, king of the bush and my wife lioness "or the brusher". My little ones, for their part, are young lions. I symbolize power, courage, and success. Many African countries use me as cultural or sportif emblem: Lions of *Teranga* for Senegalese soccer team, or Dauntless Lions for Cameroon. The young Wolofs sing to me saying:

Gayndé gayndé!

Gayndé bougoul niaxx, yapp lay doundé.

Gayndé gayndé!

Translation:

Lion, lion !

The lion does not like grass.

Lion, lion!

I can live up to 14 years in the African savannah and my wife who lives longer can reach 20 years.

Elephant

It's me Elephant. I am the most powerful animal in the African savannah. Of all the animals, my tusks are the longest and my trump the biggest. Unlike lions, tigers that are predators and carnivores, I do not hunt the weakest because I do not eat meat. I live on grass and branches, but I avoid eating the tallest and densest trees, because they allow-the forest to capture more carbon. I am a symbolic animal for many societies in Africa. For some people on the continent, I epitomize luck, power, wisdom, and experience, and for others, I am considered a very social animal and seen as a symbol of loyalty, camaraderie, and unity. I am very popular and respected in Ivory Coast, a country where I am the emblem of the national soccer team. I'm one of the animals which live longer. My life expectancy can be up to 70 years in the African bush.

The monkey

It's me monkey. Of all the animals, I'm the one who climbs the trees best. I'm half-human half-animal. I eat with my hands and carry my babies on my back. I never walk alone. I ravage the cultivated fields. This puts me in conflict with the peasants. In many traditional African tales, from Senegal to South Africa, I wear the symbolic characteristics of a cunning magician. For many Africans, I am the animal that knows the secrets of the creation of the world. I can live up to 20 years.

The Crocodile

It's me crocodile. I am also called the "river killer". I dominate what lives in water. My fangs (teeth) and my big mouth are scary. I'm not a mammal, because I lay eggs. When I get huge and threatening, they call me the "batter." Other people in Africa call me the "biter". I hold an important place in the aquatic mythology of many societies in Africa. For example, among the Baoulé people in Ivory Coast, you will often see me appearing on the carved doors, as on the weights to weigh gold where they often represent me with a fish in the jaw. I'm one of the very few animals that can live up to 100 years.

The Eagle

I am eagle, they also call me the great master of the air. My powerful greenhouses (its claws) sink into the piece of wood that serves me as a perch. Accustomed to hovering in the immense sky, I look at visitors with a grave and serious eye. I'm a raptor, a bird of prey. Like all raptors, I have been accused of all sorts of misdeeds. Some are true, some are not. One thing is certain, I am a very powerful and strategic animal. I use my strength and intelligence to catch my prey after watching them calmly from the air. For many Africans I am an unparalleled and fascinating bird. That is why I am a symbolic and emblematic animal in many African societies. I am the eponymous of African sports teams including Mali (the Eagles of Mali) and Nigeria (the Super Eagles). My lifespan is quite long, it is between 20 and 30 years.

The Turtle

I'm the turtle. In Africa, they call me fluted turtle or spur turtle. I can measure up to 80 centimeters in length for males and 50 centimeters in length for females. Males weigh about 100 kilograms and females 60 kilograms. My shell is pale beige to brown, which gives me sufficient camouflage in the sandy environment of the desert and Sahel where I prefer to live. In Africa, I am a respected symbol and emblem. In some societies, I am associated with fertility, and I represent women. In Cameroon, for example, I am a sacred animal, and no one eats my flesh because I symbolize peace, justice, and happiness. My life expectancy is about 60 years, and I can even be a hundred years old depending on the species of turtle I belong to.

The wildebeest

I'm the wildebeest. I am a large animal, and I can weigh up to 200 kilos. Despite this weight, I am one of the fastest running animals in the African savannah. I can reach a speed of 80km/h. I am a gregarious animal, that is to say I never move alone. I still live in a herd that can exceed a thousand specimens. I'm an herbivorous animal. I feed on grass, foliage, and endemic succulent plants. I can live up to 20 years. In Africa, from the savannah to the Sahel, I symbolize freedom. Africans use my horns for sculpture.

The mongoose

I'm mongoose. I live in several African countries. I am a small animal and I do not weigh more than one kilogram. Despite this, I am not a nice animal, I am even very violent. Maybe it's because I'm a carnivore, which means I grab my prey and eat them. Together with my other mongoose friends, we live in a community of 10 to 40 individuals, which, through grunting, constantly communicate and remain united. We even sleep together and follow a hierarchical system based on age. In our mongoose community, females are the ones who manage the control of the group. I can live up to 10 years.

The Gorilla

I'm gorilla. My favorite place, the African rainforest. My diet is mainly based on the consumption of foliage. In our community of gorillas, we always follow a well-defined social structure, in which the silver-backed male, its females and its offspring stand out. I am one of the few animals that uses its hands to take tools and uses them to find food. I build my own shelter and rest there with my little ones. I have a long enough life expectancy that can go up to 40 years. In the imaginary of some African peoples of the equatorial forest, such as Gabon, Equatorial Guinea, Congo, or Cameroon, I symbolize both power and shyness.

The Leopard

It's me leopard. I'm very fast. I'm a carnivore and I hunt my prey after them. My feast, I often consume it on the tree. I don't eat carriage. I leave it for hyenas and jackals. I have no friends. I don't make a lot of noise. They also call me the panther. I represent one of the emblems of power and authority in many African cultures where my skin can be the attribute of royalty, as in the Zulu community, or even compose a warlike adornment among some East African peoples. The Congo national soccer team is named after me (the Congo leopards). I can live up to 17 years.

Bustard

I'm bustard. I pass the size of the guinea fowl, but I can't reach the height of the ostrich. I fly and I run. Africans love everything about me. My feathers have several colors, and they use them to adorn hats. Hunters love my flesh. In many African societies, I symbolize successful marriage, union of souls and fertility, the descent of souls into matter. My life expectancy in the African bush can reach 23 years.

The gazelle

It's me gazelle. I am the prettiest and most charming of all animals. I run, I jump, I don't crawl. The same goes for my little ones who are called fawns. Some African children like the Fulani sing to me, saying:

Lella, Lella, ko ndogata?

Mi dogani mi diwatt?

Bidip! Bidip!

Translation

Little gazelle, little gazelle, why are you running?

I'm not running, I'm jumping.

Bidip! Bidip!

And Fulani proverb says: "lella diwaata mbiyoum sora" and the English equivalent: The apple does not fall far from the tree.

In many African savannah societies, I symbolize grace, agility, innocence. I can live up to 12 years in the bush.

The Anteater

I'm anteater. My ears resemble those of the donkey and my snout that of the pig. My tail is long, my claws are pointed. Elsewhere, they call me an aardvark. I'm a mysterious animal living on ants and termites. That is why some African societies hate me they associate me with fear and harm. The fetishists use me as an occult and dangerous power against their enemies. Therefore, I am a food ban. I can live up to 14 years in the savannah and Sahel in Africa.

The snake

I'm snake. My venom kills. My skin molts. I feed on insects, rats, and frogs. People don't dare call me by my name, especially at night. That's why they give me nicknames like "earth killer " or "crawler." In some African societies, I symbolize royal force. My life expectancy in the African environment is between 15 to 20 years in the wild and up to 30 years in captivity.

The hyena

I'm hyena. I'm a scavenger, which means I feed on the decomposing bodies of other animals. I also hunt game. I giggle and yelp. I never go alone. A lot of people talk about me in African tales of the savannah and the Sahel. Everything that's negative comes back to me. People despise me, but they're afraid of me. They don't like to say my name. They call me the "damage loveseat" or the "bushy" or even "Demba the pitiful for the adult male" or "fleeing rump". Yet, I am of great use to their environment. I clear nature of infectious debris that could spread many diseases. I can live up to 20 years in the African bush.

Ostrich

I'm Ostrich. Of all the birds, I am the tallest, the tallest of legs and my neck is the longest. I have wings, yet I don't know how to fly, but I am able to run very fast. I have beautiful feathers. Everybody covets them. Thanks to my large size and my long neck, I can see the predators approaching from a long distance, and in the savannah, I play the role of sentinel for the mixed herds of zebras and antelopes, with which we ostriches willingly mingle. I have played an important role in African societies since the dawn of time. In Ancient Egypt, my feather rose on the head of Maat goddess of justice and truth who presided over weighing of souls. My feather also served as a fair weight in the balance of judgment. As an emblem, my feather means the universal order, founded on justice. My average lifespan is very high, it amounts to 65 years in the African savannah.

The black Hippotragus

I'm black Hippotragus. They also call me the magnificent antelope. I am between 1.90 and 2.55m long, my height can reach up to 1.45m high. My weight ranges from 190 to 270kg. My tail can measure up to 75 cm. I have long horns; I am high on my feet, and I have a very long forehead. My tail looks like that of the cow, my mane like that of the horse. I'm lonely, living deep in the bush. Hunters are mean to me. My little one's name is fawn. For many specialists, I am the most beautiful antelope in the world. In countries like Angola, I am an emblematic animal. I bear the name of *Palanca negra* in Portuguese, black antelope. The players of this country's soccer team bear my name (the *Palancas negras*) (Blanc antelopes). I can live up to 20 years in the African wooded savannah especially in Mozambique, Tanzania, Zimbabwe, northern Botswana, Zambia, southern Democratic Republic of Congo, and south-eastern Angola.

The hippopotamus

I'm hippopotamus. I'm powerful. I have short legs and a big head. I prefer to be in the water because I fear the sun. I only go out at night. In Africa, they also call me the river horse. I even play an important role in biodiversity. By defecating in the rivers, I enrich them with silicon, an indispensable element for the growth of microalgae essential to the ecosystem of African rivers. In ancient African societies, I am considered as the positive symbol of pregnant women. I represent a divine figure. I can live up to 40 years.

The giraffe

I'm giraffe. I have the tallest waist of all animals. I also have the longest neck. So, I dominate all animals by my height. My anterior legs are longer than the posteriors. To eat, I stretch out my neck and pick the leaves of the trees. I'm not afraid of acacia thorns. To drink, I spread my legs and approach my head to the water. I can live up to 15 years in the bush. In traditional African societies, I represent the natural world. I am also considered the symbol of balance and harmony in the world.

The jackal

It's me jackal. I travel long distances and I move a lot. I follow in the footsteps of big animals. I feed on their leftovers. My cousin in the village is the dog. That is why in some parts of Africa I am called the "wild dog". I'm a predator of live animals. I also feed on carrions and herbs and fruits. So, I'm carnivorous and herbivorous at the same time. By finishing devouring the prey of the lions, I participate in the cleaning of the regions that I cross. I still live and move in groups or as a couple. My life expectancy is about 15 years.

The crowned crane

I'm the crowned crane. They also call me the braider's daughter. Everywhere you see me, my hair is undone and never braided. The Fulani children sing to me, they say:

Koumbâré! Koumbâré! Koumbâré mo morotako!

Koumbâré! Koumbâré! Koumbâré moraki!

Translation:

Koumbâré! Koumbâré! Koumbâré is unbraided!

Koumbâré! Koumbâré! Koumbâré is not braided!

At the Diolas of Casamance in Senegal, I am used as the effigy and symbol of the associations commonly called Jamoral which work for peace and solidarity between peoples. I can live for up to 15 years in the African savannah.

The squirrel

I'm the squirrel. I'm a rodent. In Africa, I live in burrows. I'm always on the lookout. I spend all day snooping around. As soon as something moves, I take refuge in my burrow, which has several openings. The dog and I are not friends. I am also known as the "motley one". I can live up to 15 years. In some African societies, I am a symbol of foresight, agility, liveliness, and independence. I am the emblem of the football team (soccer) of Benin, a small country that seeks to cleverly climb to the height of African football.

Lynx

I'm lynx. They also call me the little leopard of guinea fowls. I'm a big cat. I have piercing eyes. I usually go out at night and hunt chickens in villages while people sleep. In some parts of Africa, I am called "Caracal". I can live for up to 15 years in the African savannah. In many societies of the continent, I symbolize knowledge, precedence, and insight.

Zebra

I'm zebra. Some call me wild horse, others call me wild donkey. They're all right. Of all the animals, my dress is the most beautiful. My skin is covered with black and white stripes. For some societies in Africa, I symbolize courage because I undertake large annual migrations to look for pastures, despite the lions and hyenas or crocodiles that threaten me. For others, I represent cohesion, crossbreeding and harmony among peoples. I can live for up to 20 years in the African savannah.

The buffalo.

I'm buffalo. I'm powerful. I have a wide forehead and big horns, I'm scary. Of all the birds, my favorite is the beef spike, because it follows me everywhere, it accompanies me. I'm a wild bull, my female is a wild cow. In Africa, I am considered a symbol of fertility and nutrition. It's a very old belief. It started when my buffalo ancestors crossed the African landscape and the inhabitants of the areas, they had seen how their feces brought fertility to the land. I can live up to 20 years in the African bush.

The warthog

It's me warthog. They also call me the wild donkey or wild pig. My tusks look like the elephant's, but they're much smaller. They are used in particular to dig up roots or bulbs, and also to defend against my predators, lions, leopards, African wild dogs, hyenas, etc. I like to roll in the mud. I eat everything, I don't refrain myself from anything, but none dare eat my flesh. I can weigh up to 100 kilograms and my female up to 75 kilograms. My life expectancy is about 15 years. I am the symbol of sketch and brutality.

The hare

It's me hare. I'm recognized by my long ears. I'm the craftiest animal in the world and I always have plenty of tricks. In the tales of the African Sahel and savannah, I tire of the hyena with my craftiness. Whatever it is up to, I always find a solution. My teeth are sharp. I'm small and I don't have much strength. I symbolize independence, survival, and speed. For Africans and African Americans alike, I am also an unfaithful animal that represents an extreme form of behavior that people may be forced to adopt in order to survive. I can live up to 12 years depending on the species to which I belong.

The rhinoceros

I'm rhinoceros. Of all the animals, I am the ugliest, but everything I encounter stays out of my way. My legs are short, my tail too. I have a big horn on my nose and a hump on my neck. I have a very bad vision but a good sense of smell. I am very useful for fertilizing soils. I can measure 4m long by 1.50 to 2m high. I weigh a lot. My weight can reach 3 tons. There are many beliefs around my horn. That's why I'm victim of intensive poaching. Despite my life expectancy which can reach up to 50 years, I am today, an animal in danger, threatened with extinction.

The Aye-aye.

I'm aye-aye. I'm a kind of primate which lives only in Madagascar. I am a very particular lemur that can be said to combine rodent incisors, bat ears, a squirrel tail, and a particular adaptation, the third finger of my hand is extremely recumbent. I feed on insects. I am a generally solitary and nocturnal animal, discreet and difficult to observe. There are multiple legends about me. The Malagasy say that I have witchcraft powers thanks to my middle finger, an inordinate finger, used by diviners. I can live until the age of 20 in the forest of the Great African Island.

The porcupine

I'm porcupine. I'm a rodent and an herbivore. I feed on roots, bulbs, fruits, and bark. My height can reach up to 30 cm and my length 80 cm. My weight can be up to 27 kilograms. My peculiarity is my quills. They can measure up to 30 cm. They grow back after falling and become bristled when I am worried or assaulted. In the event of contact, the quills remain planted in my victim. In many African societies, I represent the symbol of untouchability. I can live up to 15 years on average.

The cobra

I'm cobra. I am a reptile that is found mainly in sub-Saharan Africa on a broad band from East Africa to West Africa. I can reach up to 2 meters in length. I feed on rodents. My venom is very powerful. When I feel threatened, I can throw venom to protect myself. This venom leads to skin irritation or even blindness when it penetrates the eyes. I have a multi-millennium history in Africa. For example, in Pharaonic Egypt, I am represented in a form that symbolized the purity of the Spiritual and Universal Vision. This is a high attribute of purity and devotion to the people, to the collective. My lifespan is 15 to 20 years in the desert, Sahel, or savannah of Africa.

The African marabout

I'm the ciconiidae. They call me the African marabout. I am a large bird with a long neck, long beak, and very long legs. I fly easily with my neck outstretched. I am recognized as an adult with a bare and hanging pocket when my neck is stretched out. I am often seen in marshes or on the shores of African lakes and rivers, but this does not mean that I am a non-water-related bird. I live and feed in the arid, open bush and wooded savannah, places where the temperature is high enough to produce air currents of heat on which I float in circles. It is when I hover that I appear in all my majesty, leg and neck extended. I am then easy to identify thanks to my large size and my massive beak. In many African societies, I am described as an aggressive, ugly, and evil bird. People say I have a serious social relationship problem. I can live up to 25 years, which is huge for a bird.

The African Python

I'm python. They also call me the python of Sheba. I am the largest python in Africa, and one of the largest snakes in the world. My length can reach up to 4 to 5 meters, sometimes even 6 meters. I weigh between 40 and 50 kg. I am not an aggressive reptile but when I am surprised or if I feel threatened or if someone tries to catch me, I am quick to bite violently. When I'm young, I feed on small mammals, birds, and frogs. As an adult, I become a dreadful predator that hunts mainly gazelles, small antelopes and young kobs, sometimes also monkeys, warthogs, damans, birds, and even young crocodiles. I kill my prey by constriction, that is, I use my muscular body to grip my victims until they are cut off or suffocated. I can be found throughout sub-Saharan Africa, all the way to the south of the Democratic Republic of Congo. I am the symbol of the Creator, and as such, I intervene in many ritual and religious ceremonies. For example, the Peda who live in South Togo and Benin worship me and consider me as their totem and the symbol of their ancestors. I can live between 15 to 20 years in the forest, the savannah, or the African Sahel.

Table of Contents

[Foreword](.) 3

[The lion](.) 4

[The elephant](.) 6

[The monkey](.) 8

[The crocodile](.) 10

[The eagle](.) 12

[The turtle :](.) 14

[The wilfebeest](.) 16

[La mongoose](.) 18

[The gorilla](.) 20

[The leopard](.) 22

[The bustard](.) 24

[The gazelle](.) 26

[The anteater](.) 28

[The snake](.) 30

[The hyena](.) 32

[The ostrich](.) 34

[Black hippotragus](.) 36

[The hippopotamus](.) 38

[The girafe](.) 40

[Le jackal](.) 42

[The crowned crane](.) 44

[The squirrel](#) 46

[The lynx](#) 48

[Thee zebra](#) 50

[Thee buffalo](#) 52

[The worthog](#) 54

[The hare](#) 56

[The rhinoceros](#) 58

[The Aye-aye.](#) 60

[Le porcupine](#) 61

[The cobra](#) 64

[The African marabout](#) 66

[The African python](#) 68

Book summary

The Africa landscapes still inspire tourists and all lovers of fauna and flora. Many animals in Africa are deeply rooted in their collective imaginary. Africa animals are distinguished by their great diversity, their incredible qualities, and their role in African societies as well as in the environment. In this book you will discover 33 animals from Africa: large and small mammals, aquatic animals, large and small birds, etc., their characteristics, their relationship with African societies as well as what they symbolize.

Author

The author is a historian with an interest in African societies, cultures, and the environment. Amadou Ba holds a PhD in History, a master's degree in Political Science and a Bachelor of Teaching degree and teaches African History at Nipissing University (North Bay ON). He is the author of four books, including: Africa of Great Empires (7th-17th centuries): 1000 Years of Economic Prosperity, Political Unity, Social Cohesion and Cultural influence; The Forgotten History of the Contribution of Slaves and Black Soldiers to Canadian Construction (1604-1945); The West African Military in the Conquest and Colonization of Madagascar 1895-1960; and John Ware (1845-1905), the Black Cowboy of Western Canada, a children's book.